NEW YORK

teNeues

NEW YORK

Photographs by Christopher Bliss
Foreword by Susan Bliss Ph.D.

teNeues

MetLife

Since the first European settlements in 1624, New York has represented freedom, hope, challenge, and excitement. It is also home to a widely diverse population. This mixture has given the city an unparalleled worldly flavor because, above all, New York is the story of the millions who walk—and have walked—its streets.

From the Statue of Liberty—Frédéric Auguste Bartholdi's gargantuan beacon that has lighted the way for generations of expectant immigrants entering New York Harbor—to the changing ethnicity of its neighborhoods, the metropolis breathes with the struggles of the people who have created its cultural enclaves and its lively commercial and artistic life.

The skyline bears witness to their tale. Architectural trends and the lifestyles that accompanied them can be traced through buildings like the 1846 Gothic style Trinity Church, the Beaux-Arts-design of Grand Central Terminal—the world's largest train station when it opened in 1913—or the quintessential example of Art-Deco, the Chrysler Building (1930). The bridges that fan out from Manhattan speak of strength and solitude.

However, structures are personalized by use and experience. The elegance of Ellis Island's French Renaissance main building is tempered by the feelings of loneliness and promise that must have overwhelmed the legions that passed through its doors. The grace of Bethesda Fountain takes on poignancy from Central Park's assurance of refuge and respite.

In the end, the place and its inhabitants can not be separated. Their histories are intertwined to paint a compelling and ongoing portrait of one of the world's most vibrant cities.

Susan Bliss Ph.D.

Seit die ersten Europäer sich 1624 hier niederließen, steht New York für Freiheit, Hoffnung, Herausforderung und ein aufregendes Leben. Die Bevölkerung der Stadt ist ausgesprochen vielfältig. Diese bunte Mischung hat New York ein unvergleichliches weltstädtisches Flair verliehen: Was diese Stadt vor allem anderen ausmacht, sind die Lebensgeschichten der Millionen von Menschen, die ihre Straßen bevölkern – und bevölkerten.

Von der Freiheitsstatue – Frédéric Auguste Bartholdis gigantischem Leuchtfeuer, das Generationen von erwartungsfrohen Einwanderern bei der Einfahrt in den Hafen von New York den Weg erhellte – bis zu den wechselnden Ethnien der Stadtviertel pulsiert die Metropole durch den Lebenskampf der Menschen, welche New Yorks kulturelle Enklaven und sein quirliges Wirtschafts- wie künstlerisches Leben geschaffen haben.

Die Skyline gibt Zeugnis von der Geschichte dieser Menschen. Die architektonischen Entwicklungen und der jeweils mit ihnen verbundene Lebensstil können an Bauwerken wie der im gotischen Stil 1846 errichteten Trinity Church, dem Jugendstilbau des Grand Central Terminal – bei seiner Eröffnung 1913 der größte Bahnhof der Welt – oder dem Chrysler Building (1930), einem idealtypischen Art-Deco-Gebäude, abgelesen werden. Die Brücken, welche Manhattan fächerförmig umgeben, drücken Strenge und Abgeschiedenheit aus.

Bauwerke erhalten jedoch durch Nutzung und Erfahrung einen individuellen Charakter. Die Eleganz des Hauptgebäudes auf Ellis Island, das im Stil der französischen Renaissance errichtet wurde, wird relativiert durch die Gefühle der Verlassenheit und der Hoffnung, die Legionen von Menschen überwältigt haben müssen, die durch seine Türen schritten. Die Anmut der Bethesda Fountain wird noch verstärkt durch das Versprechen des Central Park, Zuflucht und Ruhe zu bieten.

Letztlich sind die Stadt und ihre Einwohner nicht voneinander zu trennen. Ihre Geschichten sind ineinander verwoben und malen so ein zwingendes und stets aktuelles Porträt einer der lebendigsten Städte der Welt.

Susan Bliss Ph.D.

Depuis l'installation des premiers Européens en 1624, New York est le symbole de la liberté, de l'espoir, du défi et d'une vie palpitante. La population de la ville est extrêmement variée. Grâce à ce mélange multicolore, New York a acquis le flair incomparable d'une grande ville mondiale : Ce qui distingue cette ville avant tout, ce sont les histoires des millions de gens qui peuplent – et ont peuplé – ses rues.

De la Statue de la liberté, le gigantesque phare de Frédéric Auguste Bartholdi qui a éclairé le chemin de générations d'immigrants pleins d'espoir lors de leur arrivée au port de New York, aux ethnies changeantes des quartiers de la ville, le cœur de la métropole bat dans le combat vital des hommes qui ont créé les enclaves culturelles de New York ainsi que sa vie économique et artistique bouillonnante.

La Skyline est un témoin de l'histoire de ces individus. Les évolutions architecturales et le style de vie qui est associé à chacune d'entre elles sont visibles sur les édifices tels que la Trinity Church construite en style gothique en 1846, le bâtiment Art nouveau du Grand Central Terminal (la plus grande gare du monde lors de son inauguration en 1913) ou le Chrysler Building (1930), l'idéal de l'édifice Art Déco. Les ponts, entourant Manhattan en forme d'éventail, expriment austérité et isolement.

Les édifices obtiennent toutefois un caractère individuel en fonction de leur utilisation et de leur expérience. L'élégance de l'édifice principal d'Ellis Island, réalisé dans le style de la Renaissance française, se voit relativisée par les sentiments de solitude et d'espoir qui ont dû accabler les légions d'individus qui ont franchi ses portes. La beauté de la Bethesda Fountain se trouve renforcée par le Central Park, prometteur de refuge et de calme.

En fin de compte, la ville et ses habitants sont indissociables. Leurs histoires sont tissées l'une dans l'autre et brossent un portrait imposant et toujours actuel de l'une des villes les plus vivantes du monde.

Susan Bliss Ph.D.

Desde que los primeros europeos se asentaron aquí en 1624, Nueva York es sinónimo de la libertad, la esperanza, los desafíos y una vida excitante. La población de la ciudad es marcadamente variada. Esta mezcla variopinta ha dotado a Nueva York de un incomparable encanto cosmopolita: Lo que esta ciudad constituye sobre todo lo demás son las biografías de los millones de seres humanos que pueblan –y poblaron– sus calles.

Desde la Estatua de la Libertad –el gigantesco fuego de luz de Frédéric Auguste Bartholdi que iluminó el camino a generaciones de emigrantes expectantes a su entrada al puerto de Nueva York– hasta las etnias variables de los barrios, la metrópoli palpita a través de la lucha vital de los seres humanos que crearon los enclaves culturales de Nueva York y su despierta vida tanto económica como artística.

La skyline da testimonio de la historia de estos seres humanos. Los desarrollos arquitectónicos y el estilo de vida unido a ellos respectivamente pueden verse en edificios como la Trinity Church, erigida en 1846 en estilo gótico, el edificio modernista de la Grand Central Terminal –en su inauguración en 1913 la estación más grande del mundo– o el Chrysler Building (1930), un edificio típico ideal del art deco. Los puentes que rodean Manhattan en forma de abanico expresan rigor y aislamiento.

No obstante, los edificios reciben un carácter individual a través de la utilización y la experiencia. La elegancia del edificio principal en Ellis Island, que fue erigido en el estilo del Renacimiento francés, es relativizada por las sensaciones de abandono y esperanza que debieron vencer las legiones de seres humanos que caminaron a través de sus puertas. El encanto de la Bethesda Fountain se intensifica todavía más por la promesa del Central Park de ofrecer refugio y tranquilidad.

Al fin y al cabo, la ciudad y sus habitantes no pueden separarse. Sus historias están entretejidas entre ellas pintando así un retrato ineludible y siempre actual de una de las ciudades más llenas de vida del mundo.

Susan Bliss Ph.D.

Sin dai primi insediamenti europei nel 1624, New York è stata sinonimo di libertà, speranza, sfida e vita eccitante. E patria di una popolazione estremamente eterogenea. A tale mescolanza la città deve il suo ineguagliabile carattere di grande metropoli, poiché New York è, in primo luogo, la storia di milioni di persone che percorrono, e percorsero, le sue strade.

Dalla Statua della Libertà – il gigantesco faro di Frédéric Auguste Bartholdi che illuminò la via a generazioni di speranzosi immigranti all'entrata del porto di New York – alla mutevole etnicità dei suoi quartieri, la metropoli pulsa delle lotte della gente autrice delle sue enclavi culturali e della sua vita commerciale e artistica estremamente vive.

Lo skyline testimonia la storia di questa gente. Le tendenze architettoniche e gli stili di vita ad esse legati possono essere ripercorsi attraverso edifici quali la Trinity Church, la chiesa costruita nel 1846 in stile gotico, la costruzione Beaux Arts della Grand Central Terminal – nel 1913, all'epoca della sua inaugurazione, la stazione ferroviaria più grande del mondo – oppure il Chrysler Building (1930), un esempio di Art Deco nella sua forma più pura. I ponti che da Manhattan si aprono a ventaglio parlano di durezza e isolamento.

Attraverso l'utilizzo e l'esperienza, tuttavia, gli edifici assumono un carattere individuale. L'eleganza dell'edificio principale di Ellis Island, costruito nello stile del Rinascimento francese, è relativizzata dai sentimenti di abbandono e speranza che devono aver sopraffatto le legioni di persone che passarono per le sue porte. La grazia della Bethesda Fountain è resa più intensa dalla promessa di rifugio e sollievo di Central Park.

In fondo non è possibile separare la città dai suoi abitanti. Le loro storie s'intrecciano per dar forma ad un ritratto irresistibile e in continuo divenire di una delle città più vive del mondo.

Susan Bliss Ph.D.

WALL ST
WAY
BROADWAY
FERRIES
WALL ST

TREE
XXII
XXI
XX
XIX
XVIII
XVII
XVI
XIII
18

WATER ST
ONE WAY
An American Bistro
One of New Yorks'
Oldest Woodframe
Buildings

PIER 17

OLD FULTON ST
AFTER STOP
RIGHT TURN
PERMITTED
ON RED
ONE OLD FULTON STREET
LUNCH · DINNER
CAPPUCCINO · ESPRESSO
RESTAURANT & BAR

FUZHOU INSURANCE
福州婚姻介紹
怡發商場
紐約華人服務中心
第一駕駛學校
FOO CHOW KITCHEN

verizon

verizon

MULBERRY ST
HESTER ST
NO PARKING
BRICK-OVEN PIZZA
te Italiano
Seafood
BOLLA
BOLLA
Puglia
COCKTAIL LOUNGE
Puglia
COCKTAIL LOUNGE
Puglia
BRICK OVEN
PIZZA

YONAH SHIMMEL..
..KNISH BAKERY
Original
SINCE 1910
The Original
YONAH SCHIMMEL
KNISHERY
SPECIAL
NOW SERVING
FRESH
BAGELS
CityBusiness

KATZS
KATZ'S
That's all!
KATZ'S
LUDLOW ST
ONE
HOUSTON
WAY TO

LOW COST AUTO INSURAN
廉價汽車保險
INSURANCE
HOME
COMMERCIAL
ADVANC
Business & Services G
泰興商業資訊服
ISRAEL WHOLESALE
IMPORT CORP.
BAR MITZVAH SETS-WEDDING-GIFTS OUR SPECIALTY
SEFER TORAHS SOLD & REPAIRED
SCRIBE ON PREMISES
MENORAHS-MEZUZAS-TEFILLIN
PRAYERS SHAWLS - HEBREW BOOKS
ISRAEL WHO
BAR MITZVAH S
WHOLES
WEINFELD
SKULL CAPS
COMPANY
BENCHERS AND
YARMULKAS
TEL 212-228-4900
汽車
房屋
商業
泰興商業資訊服務中心
WWW.ABSG.BIZ
FOR RENT
Phone

15
北方鍋貼
CHINESE NORTH DUMPLING
17
ESSEX ELECTRONICS
NATAN נתן
מוצרי חשמל לארץ
110 - 220 VOLTS
אסקס אלקטרוניקס

NO PARKING

401
Broadway
BRISAS DEL CARIBE
RESTAURANT
AMERICAN FOOD
491 BROADWAY

GEORGETOWN
HOYAS

118
BLEECKER BOB'S RECORDS
LONDON
NEW YORK
HOLLYWOOD
RECORDS
475-9677
AIN • ITALY
Since 1956
N.Y.C. TAXI
5G26
TAXI FARE
118

W 9 ST
NO STANDING
TAXI
1 HOUR LIMIT
RELIEF STAND
OTHER TIMES
9L45
N.Y.C. TAXI
9L45

Union
Square
2461
New York City
Subway

CORNER
DELICATESSEN

WALKING TALL

MACYS

NYC LAW
SPEED LIMIT
30
UNLESS OTHERWISE POSTED
Herald Sq

NEW
YORKER
Pay Low...
Fly High!
Chicago

MetLife

MetLife

Times Square
THE ASTOR LIBRARY
THE LENOX LIBRARY
THE TILDEN TRUST
MDCCCXCV
THE NEW YORK PUBLIC LIBRARY

LENOX LIBRARY
FOUNDED BY
JAMES LENOX
DEDICATED TO HISTORY
LITERATURE AND THE FINE ARTS
MDCCCLXX
TILDEN TRUST
FOUNDED BY
SAMUEL JONES TILDEN
THE NEW YORK PUBLIC LIBRARY

GRAND CENTRAL
TERMINAL
ONE WAY
E 42

GRAND CENTRAL
TERMINAL

VANDERBILT HALL
INFORMATION
HARLEM LINE DEPARTURES
HARLEM LINE DEPARTURES
HUDSON LINE DEPARTURES
MTA METRO-NORTH TICKETS
SUBWAY SHUTTLE
42ND STREET
WEST BALCONY

MTA METRO-NORTH
ARRIVALS
MTA METRO-NORTH
TIMETABLES

NAT SHERMAN
MAN
E WORLD
NAT SHERMAN
TOBACCONIST TO THE WORLD

DISCOVER CARD
DISCOVER CARD
NISSIN FOODS
Budweiser
Panasonic
life today?
Be everywhere.
Be bullish.
Kodak
TIMES SQUARE GALLERY
SPECTACOLOR
Fleet
JVC
McDonald's
theatre development fund
tkts

ARGENT
Prudential
HSBC
NOVOTEL
Share Moments. Share Life.
Kodak
"I ASSURE YOU, I SERVE MY DEW FAR COLDER THAN JOHN'S. BUY YOUR DEW FROM ME!"
- ANGELO, ANGELO'S HOT DOGS
CONVENIENTLY LOCATED ACROSS THE STREET AT 44
THEATRES

42ND STREET
FORD CENTER FOR THE PERFORMING ARTS
"ABSOLUTE KNOCKOUT! LAVISH AND GLORIOUS!
BUSES
RIGHT TURNS
ONLY
7AM-10AM
4PM-7PM
MON THRU FRI
HOLIDAY SCHEDULES
42ND STREET

SUNTORY
WHISKY
Coca-Cola
REPUBLICAN
AMERICAN
NOVOTEL
Liposuction without surge
HANES SMOOTH ILLUSIONS PANTYHOSE.
The illusion is real.
JVC
TIMES SQUARE

Canon
OF THE SPIDER
WOMAN
THE MUSICAL
OLYMPUS
Real
photography.
Real
easy.
It Must Be Magic
WINNER!
7 TONY AWARDS
including
BEST
MUSICAL
BROADHURST THEATRE
What America is saving
Savings estimate since January 1990
MARTINIQUE
JEWELERS
OWARD JOHNSON'S
PLAYLAND

SPEED LIMIT 30
ONLY YOU CAN SILENCE YOURSELF
BUBBA GUMP
SHRIMP COMPANY
RESTAURANT MARKET

Sorry.
actual size.
SAMSUNG
SHERWOOD
LG
mobile phones
LG
mobile phones
AK film
WEMPE
LA CAGE
aux Folles
Pure
water
with a
hint of
flavor.

42 St

TIMES SQ
W 42 ST
ONE W
NO STANDING ANYTIME

Ask.com
Ashley Stewart
SIZES 14-26
LG
Take what
you thought
"'MAMMA MIA!' IS
ABBA-SOLUTELY
FABULOUS!"
THANK YOU FOR THE MUSIC!
MAMMA MIA!
McDonald's
Restaurant
BAR CODE
ELECTRONICS
VISTA MEDIA

HAPPY NEW YEAR
REUTERS
CUP NOODLES
NISSIN FOODS
Budweiser
Panasonic
the pure source for beautiful
Kodak
Share Moments. Share Life.™
NEW YORKERS, THERE IS AN ALTERNATIVE TO OUT-OF-TOWN RELATIVES SLEEPING ON YOUR SOFA.
NEW YORK Marriott MARQUIS
For reservations call 1-800-843-4898.
CLEARCHANNEL
MARQUIS
Millie
Fleet

PEEP
LAND
VIDEO
25¢
BOOTHS
PEEP
LAND
GIRLS
VIDEO
25¢
BOOTHS
SHOW
FOLLIES
4 THEATERS
XXX
MOVIES
PEEP LAND
LIVE GIRLS
VIDEO 25¢ BOOTHS
PEEP LAND
VIDEO BOOTH
LIVE
GIRLS
LIVE
VIDEO
25¢
OING OUT OF
SAL
PEEPLAND

LOVE
CARNEGIE
Carnegie
DELICATESSEN
RESTAURANT
TA
WE MAKE OUR OWN. PASTRIES. MEATS. PICKLES PROMPT DELIVERIES 757-2245
CARNEGIE DELICATESSEN
757-2245
GO GIANTS
Pepsi-Cola
BAKING ON THE PREMISES

RADIO CITY
MUSIC HALL
RADIO CITY
MUSIC HALL
Music Hall RADIO CITY
Music Hall RADIO CITY
PRESENTS THE 1999 CHRISTMAS SPECTACULAR STARRING THE ROCKETTES
RADIO
CITY
STOP

LANE
FIRE
BUS
NO COMMERCIAL TRAFFIC
E 57 ST

ONE WAY

BVLGARI
BUS

FedEx
Fed
FedEx DROP SLOT

BERGDORF
GOODMAN

The Plaza
MARATHON

A NEW YORK PHILHARMONIC
CHARLES

GAP
GAP

WEBER'S
WEBERS
W 71 ST
ONE WAY
NEW YORK
LOTTERY
GAMES
FREE

NYC
NYC

ESSEX
HOUSE

ESSEX
HOUSE

ANNIE LAURIE
AITKEN
GALLERIES
of
ENGLISH
DECORATIVE
ARTS
Fabergé
in America
HAUTE
COUTURE

R GUGGENHEIM MUSE
KEEP PARK CLEAN
$100,000
9K97

SUTTON EAST TENNIS CLUB

ACTIO
4518
6547
3031
3400

303
NEED

FAMOUS ORIGINAL
PIZZERIA
Coca-Cola
INDIA VALLEY
LANE
FIRE

LET
US HAVE
PEACE

THE LIBRARY OF COLUMBIA UNIVERSITY
ALMA MATER

MetLife

Christopher Bliss

As a native New Yorker, Christopher Bliss has always been drawn to the many facets of cosmopolitan life. He finds inspiration in urban skylines and in the challenging and invigorating lifestyles of cities. His work reflects the insight of a broad artistic sensibility.

Although always active in the field of photography, Chris began his career as a concert pianist, having studied both in Europe and the United States. Since 1988, he has been photographing New York as part of an ongoing project aimed at capturing the city's evolving architecture and culture. Chris's work is represented by several galleries and is part of many private and corporate collections throughout the Unites States, Canada and Europe. Several of his pieces are included in the permanent collection of the Museum of the City of New York.

Christopher Bliss

Als gebürtiger New Yorker fühlte sich Christopher Bliss seit jeher zu den zahlreichen Facetten des kosmopolitischen Lebens hingezogen. Ihn inspirieren die urbanen Skylines und die unterschiedlichen Lebensstile der Großstädte, die so herausfordernd wie belebend sind. Sein Werk spiegelt eine große künstlerische Sensibilität wider.

Obgleich Chris schon immer auf dem Gebiet der Fotografie tätig war, begann er nach dem Studium in Europa und den Vereinigten Staaten seine Karriere zunächst als Konzertpianist. Seit 1988 fotografiert er New York im Zuge eines Langzeitprojekts, dessen Ziel es ist, die Entwicklung der Architektur und Kultur dieser Stadt festzuhalten. Chris' Arbeiten werden in mehreren Galerien ausgestellt und sind in vielen privaten und öffentlichen Sammlungen in den Vereinigten Staaten, Kanada und Europa zu finden. Einige seiner Werke wurden in die Dauerausstellung des Museum of the City of New York aufgenommen.

Christopher Bliss

Né à New York, Christopher Bliss s'est toujours senti attiré par les nombreuses facettes de la vie cosmopolite. Ce qui l'inspire, ce sont les skylines urbaines et les différents styles de vie des grandes villes qui constituent des défis et qui ont à la fois un effet stimulant. Son œuvre reflète une grande sensibilité artistique.

Bien que Chris travaille depuis longtemps dans le domaine de la photographie, il a tout d'abord commencé sa carrière en tant que pianiste concertiste après avoir suivi des études en Europe et aux Etats-Unis. Depuis 1988, il photographie New York dans le cadre d'un projet à long terme dont l'objectif est d'immortaliser l'évolution de l'architecture et de la culture de cette ville. Les travaux de Chris sont exposés dans plusieurs galeries et se trouvent également dans de nombreuses collections privées et publiques aux Etats-Unis, au Canada et en Europe. Quelques-unes de ses œuvres ont été intégrées à l'exposition permanente du Museum of the City of New York.

Christopher Bliss

Habiendo nacido en Nueva York, Christopher Bliss se sintió desde siempre atraído hacia las numerosas facetas de la vida cosmopolita. Le inspiran las skylines urbanas y los diferentes estilos de vida de las grandes ciudades que son tan desafiantes como estimulantes. Su obra refleja una gran sensibilidad artística.

Aunque Chris siempre había trabajado en el campo de la fotografía, inició su carrera primero como concertista de piano después de sus estudios en Europa y en los Estados Unidos. Desde 1988 fotografía Nueva York en el curso de un proyecto a largo plazo cuyo objetivo es fotografiar la evolución de la arquitectura y la cultura de esta ciudad. Los trabajos de Chris se exponen en varias galerías y pueden encontrarse en muchas colecciones privadas y públicas en los Estados Unidos, Canadá y Europa. Algunas de sus obras fueron acogidas en la exposición permanente del Museum of the City of New York.

Christopher Bliss

Newyorkese di nascita, Christopher Bliss è sempre stato attratto dalle numerose sfaccettature della vita cosmopolita. Egli trae ispirazione dagli skyline urbani e dai diversi stili di vita, tanto provocatori quanto stimolanti, delle grandi città. Le sue opere rispecchiano una grande sensibilità artistica.

Pur avendo sempre lavorato nel campo della fotografia, Chris ha iniziato la sua carriera come pianista da concerti, dopo aver studiato in Europa e negli Stati Uniti. Dal 1988 si dedica alla realizzazione di fotografie di New York come parte di un progetto in divenire inteso a catturare l'evoluzione dell'architettura e della cultura di questa città. I lavori di Chris vengono esposti in varie gallerie e si ritrovano in molte collezioni private e pubbliche negli Stati Uniti, in Canada e in Europa. Alcune sue opere sono entrate a fare parte della mostra permanente del Museum of the City of New York.

Indice delle materie   Directory   Verzeichnis   Table des matières   Directorio

Front cover: Aerial view of Manhattan looking north
Back cover: Brooklyn Bridge in the rain

www.newyorkpictures.com

Photographs by Christopher Bliss
Design by Diana Morrow, teNeues Publishing
Introduction by Susan Bliss Ph.D.
Translation by SAW Communications,
Dr. Sabine A. Werner, Mainz
Heike Rosbach (German)
Céline Verschelde (French)
Gemma Correa-Buján (Spanish)
Elena Nobilini (Italian)
Editorial coordination by Christina Burns,
teNeues Publishing
Production by Sandra Jansen, teNeues Verlag
Color separation by O/R/T/ Medienverbund, Krefeld

Bibliographic information published by Die Deutsche Bibliothek. Die Deutsche Bibliothek lists this publication in the Deutsche Nationalbibliographie; detailed bibliographic data is available in the Internet at http://dnb.ddb.de

ISBN-10: 3-8327-9033-0
ISBN-13: 978-3-8327-9033-2

Printed in Italy

Published by teNeues Publishing Group

teNeues Book Division
Kaistraße 18
40221 Düsseldorf
Germany
Phone: 00 49-(0)2 11-99 45 97-0
Fax: 00 49-(0)2 11-99 45 97-40
e-mail: books@teneues.de
Press department: arehn@teneues.de
Phone: 00 49-(0) 21 52-916-202

teNeues Publishing Company
16 West 22nd Street
New York, N.Y. 10010
USA
Phone: 001-212-627-9090
Fax: 001-212-627-9511

teNeues Publishing UK Ltd.
P.O. Box 402
West Byfleet
KT14 7ZF
Great Britain
Phone: 0044-1932-403509
Fax: 0044-1932-403514

teNeues France S.A.R.L.
4, rue de Valence
75005 Paris
France
Phone: 00 33-1-55 76 62 05
Fax: 00 33-1-55 76 64 19

teNeues Iberica S.L.
c/ Velázquez 57 6.° izda.
28001 Madrid
Spain
Phone: 00 34-65 71 32 133

teNeues Representative Office Italy
Via San Vittore 36/1
20123 Milano
Italy
Phone: 00 39 (0) 347 76 40 551

www.teneues.com

teNeues Publishing Group
Kempen
Düsseldorf
London
Madrid
Mailand
New York
Paris

teNeues